READ & RESPOND

Helping children discover the pleasure and power of reading

LIBBY SCOTT & REBECCA WESTCOTT

CAN
expected to
YOU
fit in
SEE
proud to
ME?
STAND OUT

FOR AGES 9–11

Published in the UK by Scholastic Education, 2023

Scholastic Distribution Centre, Bosworth Avenue, Tournament Fields, Warwick, CV34 6UQ

Scholastic Ireland, 89E Lagan Road, Dublin Industrial Estate, Glasnevin, Dublin, D11 HP5F

SCHOLASTIC and associated logos are trademarks and/or registered trademarks of Scholastic Inc.

© 2023 Scholastic

www.scholastic.co.uk

1 2 3 4 5 6 7 8 9   3 4 5 6 7 8 9 0 1 2

A CIP catalogue record for this book is available from the British Library.
ISBN 978-0702-31956-3

Printed and bound by Ashford Colour Press
This book is made of materials from well-managed,
FSC®-certified forests and other controlled sources.

MIX
Paper from
responsible sources
FSC® C011748

Authors Louise Dobson
Editorial team Rachel Morgan, Vicki Yates, Suzanne Adams, Helen Cox Cannons
Series designer Andrea Lewis
Typesetter QBS Learning
Illustrator Rhiannon Archard

Acknowledgements
The publishers gratefully acknowledge permission to reproduce the following material:
Scholastic Children's Books for the use of the text extracts and cover from *Can You See Me?* written by Libby Scott and Rebecca Westcott.
The Big Issue for the use of 'Libby Scott: "My autism diagnosis stopped me hating myself"' as first published in The Big Issue.
Every effort has been made to trace copyright holders for the works reproduced in this book, and the publishers apologise for any inadvertent omissions.

For supporting online resources go to:
www.scholastic.co.uk/read-and-respond/books/can-you-see-me/online-resources
Access key: Provide

CONTENTS ▼

How to use Read & Respond in your classroom...

Read & Respond provides teaching ideas related to a specific well-loved children's book. Each Read & Respond book is divided into the following sections:

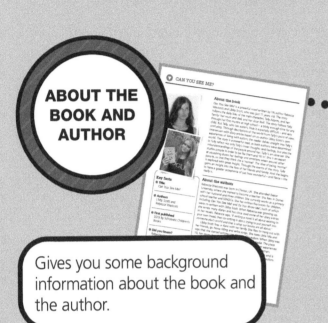

ABOUT THE BOOK AND AUTHOR

Gives you some background information about the book and the author.

GUIDED READING

Breaks the book down into sections and gives notes for using it, ideal for use with the whole class. A bookmark has been provided on page 12 containing **comprehension** questions. The children can be directed to refer to these as they read. Find comprehensive guided reading sessions on the supporting online resources.

SHARED READING

Provides extracts from the children's book with associated notes for focused work. There is also one non-fiction extract that relates to the children's book.

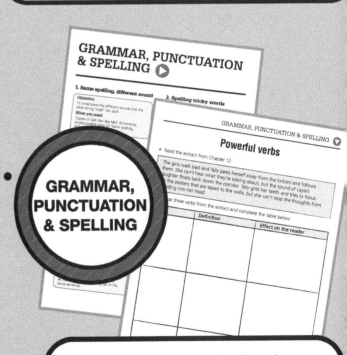

GRAMMAR, PUNCTUATION & SPELLING

Provides word-level work related to the children's book so you can teach grammar, punctuation, spelling and **vocabulary** in context.

PLOT, CHARACTER & SETTING

Contains activity ideas focused on the plot, characters and the setting of the story.

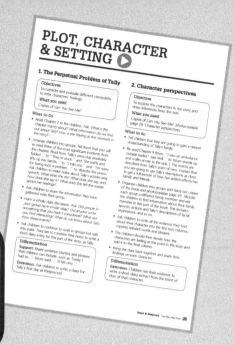

TALK ABOUT IT

Oracy, **fluency**, and speaking and listening activities. These activities may be based directly on the children's book or be broadly based on the themes and concepts of the story.

GET WRITING

Provides writing activities related to the children's book. These activities may be based directly on the children's book or be broadly based on the themes and concepts of the story.

ASSESSMENT

Contains short activities that will help you assess whether the children have understood concepts and curriculum objectives. They are designed to be informal activities to feed into your planning.

SUPPORTING ONLINE RESOURCE

Online you can find a host of supporting documents including planning information, comprehensive guided reading sessions and guidance on teaching reading.

www.scholastic.co.uk/read-and-respond/books/can-you-see-me/online-resources
Access key: Provide

Help children develop a love of reading for pleasure.

Activities

The activities follow the same format:

- **Objective:** the objective for the lesson. It will be based upon a curriculum objective, but will often be more specific to the focus being covered.

- **What you need:** a list of resources you need to teach the lesson, including photocopiable pages.

- **What to do:** the activity notes.

- **Differentiation:** this is provided where specific and useful differentiation advice can be given to support and/or extend the learning in the activity. Differentiation by providing additional adult support has not been included as this will be at a teacher's discretion based upon specific children's needs and ability, as well as the availability of support.

The activities are numbered for reference within each section and should move through the text sequentially – so you can use the lesson while you are reading the book. Once you have read the book, most of the activities can be used in any order you wish.

CURRICULUM LINKS

Section	Activity	Curriculum objectives
Guided reading		Comprehension: To maintain positive attitudes to reading and understanding of what they read.
Shared reading	1	Comprehension: To discuss and evaluate how authors use language, including figurative language, considering the impact on the reader.
	2	Comprehension: To draw inferences such as inferring characters' feelings, thoughts and motives from their actions, and to justify inferences with evidence.
	3	Comprehension: To identify and discuss themes and conventions in and across a wide range of writing.
	4	Comprehension: To retrieve, record and present information from non-fiction.
Grammar, punctuation & spelling	1	Transcription: To understand that…the spelling of some words needs to be learnt specifically, as listed in English Appendix 1.
	2	Transcription: To understand that…the spelling of some words needs to be learnt specifically, as listed in English Appendix 1.
	3	Comprehension: To explain the meaning of words in context.
	4	Composition: To integrate dialogue to convey character and advance the action.
	5	Composition: To recognise vocabulary…appropriate for formal speech and writing.
	6	Comprehension: To identify how language, structure and presentation contribute to meaning.
Plot, character & setting	1	Spoken language: To consider and evaluate different viewpoints. Comprehension: To draw inferences such as inferring characters' feelings, thoughts and motives from their actions, and to justify inferences with evidence.
	2	Comprehension: To draw inferences such as inferring characters' feelings, thoughts and motives from their actions, and to justify inferences with evidence.
	3	Comprehension: To participate in discussions about books; to draw inferences such as inferring characters' feelings, thoughts and motives from their actions, and to justify inferences with evidence.
	4	Comprehension: To draw inferences such as inferring characters' feelings, thoughts and motives from their actions, and to justify inferences with evidence.
	5	Comprehension: To make comparisons within and across books.
	6	Comprehension: To discuss and evaluate how authors use language, including figurative language, considering the impact on the reader; to prepare poems…to read aloud.
	7	Comprehension: To identify how language, structure and presentation contribute to meaning.
	8	Comprehension: To ask questions to improve understanding of a text.

Section	Activity	Curriculum objectives
Talk about it	1	Spoken language: To participate in role play and improvisations.
	2	Spoken language: To participate in role play and improvisations.
	3	Spoken language: To maintain attention and participate actively in collaborative conversation, staying on topic and initiating and responding to comments.
	4	Spoken language: To articulate and justify answers, arguments and opinions.
	5	Spoken language: To ask relevant questions to extend their understanding and knowledge.
	6	Spoken language: To participate in presentations.
Get writing	1	Composition: To identify the audience for and purpose of the writing.
	2	Composition: To integrate dialogue to convey character and advance the action.
	3	Composition: To select appropriate grammar and vocabulary, understanding how such choices can change and enhance meaning.
	4	Composition: To identify the audience for and purpose of the writing; to use organisational and presentational devices to structure texts.
	5	Composition: To select appropriate grammar and vocabulary, understanding how such choices can change and enhance meaning.
	6	Composition: In writing narratives, to consider how authors have developed characters and settings in what they have read, listened to or seen performed.
Assessment	1	Spoken language: To listen and respond appropriately.
	2	Comprehension: To discuss their understanding and explore the meaning of words in context.
	3	Comprehension: To discuss and evaluate how authors use language.
	4	Comprehension: To draw inferences such as inferring characters' feelings, thoughts and motives from their actions, and to justify inferences with evidence.
	5	Comprehension: To listen and respond appropriately; to summarise the main ideas drawn from more than one paragraph, identifying key details that support the main ideas.
	6	Composition: In narratives, to describe settings, characters and atmosphere.

CAN YOU SEE ME?

Key facts

◉ **Title:**
Can You See Me?

◉ **Authors**
Libby Scott and
Rebecca Westcott

◉ **First published**
2019 by Scholastic Children's
Books

◉ **Did you know?**
Rebecca says that the minute
she began working with
Libby she knew that they
would have the opportunity
to create something
very special.
Libby has a dog called Louie,
who is not only super-cute,
but also helps her when she
is feeling anxious.

About the book

Can You See Me? is a powerful novel written by YA author Rebecca Westcott and Libby Scott, who was just 11 years old. The story follows the daily lives of the main character, Tally Adams, and her family: her mum and dad, and her sister Nell. The story follows Tally through her first months at high school – a tricky enough time for any child. But Tally, who has autism, finds it especially difficult – and very confusing. Through descriptions of the world from Tally's point of view, interwoven with diary entries based on co-author Libby Scott's own experiences of living with autism, the reader delves straight into Tally's world. The story is a powerful read, as both authors were determined to fully reflect not only Tally's inner thoughts and feelings, but also the misunderstandings of the people around her. Tally is an observer. She studies people in order to be like them and 'fit in'. She is an expert at squashing down her feelings and emotions when around other people, so that they think she is 'normal'. The idea of being 'normal' is explored with great insight. Through the events of the story, Tally gains an insight into the lives of her friends and family. And she begins to have a greater acceptance of just how wonderful – and fierce – she really is.

About the authors

Rebecca Westcott was born in Chester, UK. She attended Exeter University, where she trained to become a teacher. She lives in Dorset with her husband and three children. She currently works as a primary school teacher and SENDCo. She has written five books for children, including *Can You See Me?* and *Do You Know Me?*, both of which were co-written with Libby Scott. When Rebecca was growing up, she wrote many diaries and has since used some of her diary entries in her novels. Rebecca says, 'If writing a novel is all about existing in your own head, then co-writing is about trying to put yourself into someone else's world and that is what our books are all about.'

Libby Scott lives in Kent with her family. She likes to hang out with her friends, go horse riding and write songs. She loves Little Mix and says that she started writing one day out of boredom. When Libby was 10, her mum shared some of her writing on social media. The piece was entitled, 'Life as a Perfectionist'. She wrote about her experiences of living with autism, along with advice for parents and teachers. Libby is passionate about sharing her experiences with others and is especially keen to smash the many stereotypes that surround autism.

GUIDED READING ▶

Introduction – before reading

Introduce the book by reading the title. Ask: *What does this question make you think about?* Explore the words in between the main title – 'Expected to Fit in PROUD to STAND OUT'. Ask: *What does 'fitting in' mean? Can you think of any examples? Is it important to 'fit in'? Is your answer different if you think about different places, such as at home, at school or on holiday?* Then explore 'standing out' together – what might this mean? Ask: *When might someone be proud to 'stand out'?*

Talk to the children about the two authors. Explain that the book was written as a collaboration between the author, Rebecca Westcott, and Libby Scott – who was 11 years old at the time. Libby has autism and often writes about her experiences.

Chapters 1 to 4

Briefly set the scene for children. Ask: *What feelings do you have at the end of the summer holidays?* If teaching Year 6 children, encourage them to discuss how they think they will feel during the next summer, when they know that high/secondary school is approaching.

After reading Chapters 1 and 2, ask: *What information can you share about the main character, Tally?* Encourage them to give evidence from the text to support their ideas. (She likes feeling close to the sky, she feels 'weightless and free'; she is worried about high school; she loves the fair, especially the haunted house.) *What have we learned about her sister, Nell?* (She is fourteen, she shares Tally's love of the haunted house.) We begin to learn a little about Tally's autism with her first diary extract and list of 'autism facts'. Explain to the children that the diary entries are based on Libby Scott's own diaries that were published on social media by her mum. Ask: *Why do you think that writing about her autism is important to Libby?* This could be a very sensitive subject to some children in the class, but it may be interesting to ask if some children would like to share their experiences. After reading Chapters 3 and 4, ask: *What new information have we learned about Tally?*

Chapters 5 to 8

Read Chapter 5, modelling fluency and expression. Model a change of expression when reading the diary entry and the 'autism factsheet' and discuss the difference with the children. Discuss question 8 on the Guided reading bookmark. Ask children for their initial thoughts about the drama teacher, Mrs Jarman. Ask: *Why does Tally wince when Mrs Jarman claps?* (She has heightened senses.) Ask: *Can you explain why Mrs Jarman is confusing to Tally? What do you think about Mrs Jarman's 'Top Tips' box?* (Check they understand the sarcasm used by the teacher.) *What adjectives does Tally use to describe her meltdowns?* ('terrifying', 'frightening') *How does Tally feel afterwards?* ('isolated, guilty', 'like everyone's against her') *What helps Tally to calm down?* (her mum, doing a favourite thing) Read Chapters 6 and 7 together. Ask: *How does the fair smell to Tally?* ('mysterious and hot and dangerous') *Why 'dangerous'?*

Read the beginning of Chapter 8, up to the part where Mrs Jarman enters the drama studio. Ask children to predict how Mrs Jarman will react to Tally being in the studio. They could jot notes in their notebook. Read to the end of the chapter and compare children's predictions.

Chapters 9 to 11

Read Chapter 9. It is in this chapter that the reader gets a deeper insight into one of Tally's meltdowns. We can gradually see Tally's meltdown building throughout the scene. Ask: *What clues do we have for how frustrated Tally is becoming during this scene?* (Tally thinks she has asked nicely for orange juice; her dad gives her mum 'a look' that Tally can't interpret – she feels 'confused'; Dad's face goes red 'like a traffic light' and this signals to Tally to 'STOP' but she can't...) Ask the children if they have heard of 'stimming' and to explain it in their own words. Explore children's thoughts about this moment in the story.

Read Chapters 10 and 11. In Chapter 10, Tally considers the difference between herself and Nell, when they are in trouble with their mum. Nell says to Tally, 'It wouldn't have killed you to say sorry too'. Ask: *Why does Tally believe that she is saying sorry?* (She is eating the toast like her mum told her to.)

Read Chapter 11. Refer to question 10 on the bookmark. Ask: *Why does Tally begin to walk more slowly?* (She takes Nell literally when she asks her, 'Is it possible for you to walk any slower?') *How is Nell feeling at this point of the story? What does Tally find on the pavement?* (the worm again) *What is the forbidden word that Nell uses?* (tantrum) *Why does this word upset Tally so much?* (This is explained earlier, in Chapter 5.)

Chapters 12 to 17

Read Chapter 12. Discuss question 11 on the bookmark. The 'rule of three' (where three words or phrases are used to describe something) is used throughout the book – suggest that children note examples as they read to use later in their writing. Ask: *In what ways are the girls' changing rooms 'too much' for Tally?* (They are an overload on her senses.) Ask: *How does Tally describe the pain she feels?* ('Her body feels like it's on fire…it feels like a needle or a pin…') Refer to question 3 on the bookmark. Direct children to the final paragraphs: 'But she does not stop…Even if it hurts more than you can tell them.' Together, explore why this piece is particularly powerful.

After reading Chapters 13 and 14, explore Tally's encounter with Rupert, Mrs Jessop's three-legged dog. Tally has an 'important conversation' to have with Rupert. Tally is incredibly empathetic towards Rupert. Tally asks Rupert, 'Can you see me?' – the title of the book. They are both wearing 'masks'. Ask: *Why would it be important for the writers to show Tally's relationship with Rupert (and the worm)?* Answer question 7 on the bookmark.

Ask: *In Chapter 14, what is happening between Nell and the two high-school girls?* This incident is not fully explained to the reader. Refer to question 13 on the bookmark. *What can we infer? What do you think has happened?* (Is Nell being bullied because her sister is 'different'?) *How is Nell feeling at this point in the story? What evidence from the story backs up your answers?*

Read Chapters 15 to 17. In Chapter 15, Tally tries to 'fit in' at the sleepover – ask: *Why did Tally research sleepovers before she went to Layla's house?* (She says that it is 'very important that she is normal for the next eighteen hours and thirty minutes'.) *How do things go wrong for Tally?* (She's overwhelmed by the makeover, does not like the food, is scared by the film, misses her cuddly toy.) In this part of the story, Tally shows a huge amount of strength. Ask: *How does Tally describe how her friends are making her feel?* (She feels like she is '… clinging on to the side of a cliff while her friends all peel her fingers off the edge, one at a time.').

Answer question 2 on the bookmark, referring to the end of Chapter 16. Ask children for their thoughts on the main event in Chapter 17, Luke stealing the assessment paper. Ask: *How do Tally's friends react when she enters the classroom? How does Luke react? What is happening that Tally does not understand?* Ask children to consider question 14 on the bookmark.

Chapters 18 to 20

Ask children to consider why Tally tells Mr King that it was Luke who stole the assessment paper.

Initial ideas can be noted and displayed – what do children think about the idea of 'normal' – and what is normal? Ask children to answer question 15 on the bookmark. Then refer to question 5.

Ask: *How do Tally's friends treat Tally towards the end of Chapter 20? Why? What goes horribly wrong for Tally?* When reading the final part of Chapter 20, ask children how this makes them, as a reader, feel. (It's very uncomfortable reading as Tally had forgotten about Luke's mum leaving him and his dad when he was at primary school.)

Chapters 21 and 22

Ask children to consider why Luke is late to the drama class. (There are rumours that he has had a fight with a Year 10 pupil.) Encourage children to make connections between this knowledge and the events of the previous chapter. Ask: *How did you react when Mrs Jarman read out Tally's latest Top Tip? What is the understanding that Tally arrives at towards the end of Chapter 21?* Explore the final line of the chapter: 'What if she isn't the only one?' This is a particularly powerful moment in the story. Ask children what they think about this. Ask: *Is Tally not the only one?*

After reading Chapter 22, ask: *What similarities does Tally feel she shares with Rupert?* Consider the advice that Tally gives Rupert, and link this to Tally's recent experiences.

Chapters 23 to 25

Ask children to answer question 4 on the bookmark and then read Chapter 23. Ask: *Why does Tally take the mask to school with her?* (It comforts her.) Tally doesn't immediately understand what she is seeing in the middle of the room. Encourage children to view the scene from Tally's point of view ('He has taken her one good thing and ruined it for ever'), and then the point of view of the rest of the children in the class ('It was supposed to be a laugh…'). Sensitively explore what happens next when Tally is overloaded and cannot cope; how she relates the looks on the faces of her classmates with the looks that her family gives to Rupert. Reflect on your discussions of the earlier chapters about Rupert. These chapters are particularly emotional – you will be the best judge of how to approach events with your class. One idea would be to ask children to write down any thoughts/feelings/ideas/questions that they have on a piece of paper and post them (anonymously or not) in a box similar to the 'Top Tips' box. These can then be addressed during a whole class discussion.

After reading Chapter 24, ask: *How does Mrs Jarman help Tally to feel better? What advice does she give her?*

After reading Chapter 25, answer question 9 on the bookmark. Ask: *What words and phrases are used to describe how Tally feels just before she experiences her meltdown?* ('…as if it isn't words that are coming out of his mouth but a swarm of angry wasps…The buzzing turns into a roaring sound, louder than a whole ambush of tigers') Answer question 12 on the bookmark. Then discuss question 16 on the bookmark.

Chapters 26 and 27

Ask: *Why does Tally refuse to go to the hospital with her mum and Nell?* ('Her body is empty, like a car without any fuel and her head is filled with a swirling, cloudy terror…')

After reading Chapter 27, ask: *What does Tally insist that she and Nell do?* (find Rupert) *What does she think about Rupert at this point in the story?* (He knows what it feels like 'to be different' and to have 'no one understand you'.) Tally links her own experiences to Rupert and is able to work out where he has gone. Answer question 6 on the bookmark.

Chapters 28 to 30

After reading Chapter 28, ask: *Why does Tally get a 'swooshing feeling' when Rupert nudges her leg with his nose?* (It's a feeling of love/a connection.) *How does Tally feel in the hospital? How does Nell help her?* (She reminds Tally how brave she was in the dark when looking for Rupert, Nell has brought her tiger mask to the hospital.) *Tally lists all the things that Tiger Girl doesn't do – what are they?* (run away when scared, flap her hands, make weird noises). Ask: *What are Tally's dreams for the future?*

Read to the end of the book. Ask the children why Tally is so happy in the final chapter (Rupert can stay). Tally worries that her sister doesn't understand her any more. Ask: *What two things happen that help to put Tally's mind at ease about her sister and about going back to school?* (She sees Nell place a worm onto the grass verge and Aleksandra greets her as she walks towards school). *How do you feel about the ending of the story?* Discuss question 1 on the bookmark.

Can You See Me?

by Libby Scott and Rebecca Westcott

Focus on...
Meaning

1. How would you describe the main theme of the book?

2. List some of the 'Pros' and 'Cons' that Tally explains about her autism.

3. Why does Tally continue to run in her PE lesson, even when her foot is hurting her?

4. Why does Tally wear the tiger mask? What does it mean to her?

5. The word 'normal' is mentioned many times in the book. What does this mean to Tally?

6. Describe Tally's thoughts and feelings about Rupert. Why have the writers chosen to include Rupert in the story?

Focus on...
Organisation

7. Why does the story use extracts from Tally's diary?

8. What do 'Tally's autism facts' add to the story?

Can You See Me?

by Libby Scott and Rebecca Westcott

Focus on...
Language and features

9. What does the simile '…like a jigsaw piece that is in the wrong puzzle box' mean to you? What does it tell you about how Tally is feeling at this moment in time?

10. Consider the effect of the use of repetition in Chapter 11: '…difficult men and difficult dogs and difficult children.'

11. Can you find any examples of the 'rule of three' in Chapter 12?

12. Talk about the effects of the metaphors used in Chapter 25.

Focus on...
Purpose, viewpoints and effects

13. How does Nell feel in Chapter 14?

14. Why does Luke call Tally 'Weirdo Adams' throughout the story? What is the effect on Tally?

15. In Chapter 19, how do the waiter and the other people in the restaurant view Tally's behaviour? Why?

16. How does 'masking' help Tally? What are the 'cons' of masking?

SHARED READING ▶

Extract 1

- Read the Extract 1 to the children, demonstrating fluent and expressive reading.

- Follow this up with an echo-reading activity, where you read a passage from the extract and ask the class to read it back in exactly the same way. For this, choose particularly effective passages such as 'Up where the sky begins… possibilities are endless.' and 'It is a final-days-of-summer kind of afternoon…completely normal family.'

- Ask pairs to talk about the extract, relating it to their own experiences. Display these questions to focus their conversations:

  ○ Do you have a special place where you go to feel calm and safe?

  ○ Do you ever look at the sky?

  ○ What do you think about it?

  ○ Do you prefer the sky in the day, or a night sky? Explain your answer.

- Explore how Tally feels when she is on the roof of the shed.

- Explain that there is a lot of repetition used in the extract – allow time for children to find examples of this and then discuss the effect. For example, the word 'up' is repeated. Being close to the sky seems very important to Tally. Ask: Which words/phrases from the text suggest this? ('possibilities are endless', 'only rule', she feels 'fierce and brave') The word 'normal' is repeated. Ask children what they think about the sentence: 'It's funny how if you say it enough times, the word normal sounds anything but'. Ask: Have you ever experienced this when saying a familiar word? What does the writer mean by this? Does Tally feel like a normal girl?

- Explain that the sky is often described in the story and this will be explored in future activities.

Extract 2

- Model reading Extract 2 with fluency and expression, paying particular attention to the dialogue. For example, read Ayesha's words in a voice that is 'quiet and a bit shaky' and make Lucy's words sound 'fierce'.

- Write these three words on the board: 'flanked', 'huddles', 'overwhelming'. Ask the children to find and circle these words in the extract. Explain each word using everyday language, for example, 'at the side of', 'close together', 'too much'.

- Together, complete the Focus word table from the supporting online resource (see page 5). Example sentences could be: 'The criminal was flanked by many police officers', 'Penguins huddle together for warmth', 'The music and lights at the disco were overwhelming'. Provide a definition for each word in the final column and discuss these together.

- Play 'Have you ever?' with the children by asking them to discuss the following with a partner:

  ○ Have you ever experienced something overwhelming?

  ○ Have you ever been flanked by something/someone?

  ○ Have you ever huddled?

- Share children's ideas.

- Ask children to create and record a sentence in their book for each of the focus words.

- Return to the extract and re-read it together, using choral reading. Before reading, ask children to be on the lookout for the focus words. Explore the text around each focus word and ask children to describe, in their own words, what is happening. Encourage the children to use their knowledge of the focus words to give explicit meaning to events in the text.

Extract 3

- Hand out Extract 3. Read through the text, modelling reading with expression – showing Tally's growing frustration with the waiter and her worried thoughts about seeing her friends when she was wearing her mask.

- Ask children to circle each of the characters involved in this extract. Share all ideas and write a list on the board:
  - Tally
  - Mum, Dad, Nell
  - The waiter
  - The family of five, including 'the mother' and people at the table behind.

- Split the class into four groups and ask each group to focus on one of the above characters/ groups. Ask children to re-read the extract and to highlight any dialogue and description for their character/s only.

- Then, ask children to write notes in the margin on their character's/characters' thoughts and feelings at this point in the story. They have to put themselves in the characters' 'shoes'.

- Ask children to consider *why* their characters may be thinking and feeling these things. Ask: *What evidence can we find to show the reasons behind their actions (motive)?* An example you can share is: '"That child needs to be taught some manners," tuts the mother…'. The mother and her family witness Tally shouting at her dad and the waiter. The 'sniffing' is showing that the family are shocked to see a child behave this way in public. This is shown by the way they stare at Tally. Tally then 'yells' at the family. The mother assumes that Tally is a naughty girl who needs to be disciplined. She tuts, showing her disgust. She will have no idea that Tally is autistic.

- Bring the class back together to share ideas, noting them on the board.

Extract 4

- Hand out Extract 4. Inform children that this extract is based on an interview that the young author, Libby Scott, had with a magazine called The *Big Issue*. Give a little background information on the interview: it is about Libby receiving her diagnosis of autism.

- Read the extract together and ask questions to gauge children's initial understanding: *How did Libby first feel when she received her diagnosis? What did she worry about at first? How does Libby explain how the diagnosis helped her to not hate herself? What is 'the special gang' that Libby wasn't a part of before? What does Libby recommend to parents who are worried that their child may have autism?*

- Ask: *What is the purpose of this piece of writing? What kind of text is it? Who is it aimed at? Is the text sharing facts or opinion?* Discuss together how the purpose is to inform readers of The *Big Issue* about the experiences of a young girl with autism. It is based on her personal experiences but will also be of interest to parents, as well as children and young adults. It is an interview, so we learn about the feelings and experiences of the person being interviewed – Libby Scott. It is sharing the opinions of Libby.

- Ask: *What have you learned about Libby Scott?* Encourage the children to use what they now know about Libby and consider questions that they would like to ask about her. Ask: *How do your questions reflect what we already know?*

Extract 1

Look up. Go on, do it now. Stretch back your neck and stare up, as far as you can. And then a little bit more. That's where you're going to have to look if you want to find Tally Olivia Adams. Up where the sky begins. Up where the only rule is gravity. Up where the world seems small and not so important. Up where the possibilities are endless.

It is a final-days-of-summer kind of afternoon. Fluffy white clouds are scudding across the pale blue sky and the air has a hint of something fresh, something new. A normal day on a normal street in the back garden of a normal house belonging to a completely normal family.

Read that last sentence again, out loud to yourself. It's funny how if you say it enough times, the word normal sounds anything but.

So, a normal day. But the girl standing on the roof of the garden shed is not normal in the slightest. She is a warrior, fierce and brave, surveying the land before her. She's a mountain climber, pausing for breath after scaling the heady heights of Everest. She is a trapeze artist, about to step out on to the wire and dazzle the crowds beneath her.

Her right foot rises in the air, shaking slightly as she contemplates the drop. One wrong move and it will all be over.

"Hey! Get down!"

The shout makes Tally wobble and for a split second it seems as if she will tumble to earth. But then her foot makes contact with the roof and she lowers herself to the ridge, sitting with her legs dangling out in front of her.

"You nearly made me fall." Tally glares at Nell accusingly. "Are you trying to kill me?"

Extract 2

Tally's stomach starts to churn. Nell promised her that she'd be fine at Kingswood Academy. She certainly didn't say anything about bullying or people being unkind or *things going on*. She isn't sure what that is supposed to mean but it doesn't sound good.

They reach the steps and the girls close in around her. For a second, Tally imagines that she's a celebrity being flanked by her bodyguards. This is probably how Taylor Swift feels, every single time she steps outside her house.

"Don't worry, OK?" Ayesha's voice sounds quiet and a bit shaky as they climb the first step. "You're bound to get lost and feel a bit scared to begin with but I'm sure all the teachers will be really nice."

Lucy's face is set in a fierce-looking expression. "There's really nothing to be scared about." She slows down as they move upwards.

"We're right here with you. Nobody can hurt you when we're all together." Layla's hand tightens on Tally's arm as they reach the top.

Suddenly Tally is at the front of the group, leading the way as they push through the doors and into the building. And she wonders how they can all be so brave when what she really wants to do, now that she's been told about the scary things that might happen and the possibility of getting lost, is to run in the opposite direction.

There are teachers waiting inside, directing them all towards the hall. Tally huddles closer to her friends as everyone starts to push and shove their way down the corridor. The noise is overwhelming and she squeezes her fists tightly as she stares straight ahead, hoping that if she doesn't look at the crowds then it might be easier.

Extract 3

"Why don't you choose the burger?" suggests Mum. "I'm sure that we could ask for it to be served without the relish or the gherkins?"

"Certainly, Madam," says the waiter.

"But I want toast," repeats Tally. "I don't want a burger."

"And as I said, we don't offer toast." The waiter gives Tally a hard look. "We can adapt any item on the menu but you cannot order a meal that we don't actually offer."

"Look, Tally, how about you—" begins Dad but Tally doesn't let him finish.

"I want a piece of toast!" she shouts. "Plain, white toast with nothing on it. That's the easiest thing in the entire world to cook, even I can make it at home – so why can't I have it here?"

There is a sniffing sound from the next table and when Tally glances over, she sees the entire family of five staring at her. It reminds her of the way that her so-called friends were staring at her outside McDonalds.

"It's rude to stare!" she yells. "Didn't anyone ever teach you that?"

"That child needs to be taught some manners," tuts the mother, and the people at the table behind her nod in agreement.

"Give her two days living in my house and she wouldn't be behaving like that out in public," mutters another woman. "I blame the parents. They're incapable of disciplining their children these days."

Extract 4

Libby Scott: 'My autism diagnosis stopped me hating myself'

When you received the diagnosis, how did you feel?

I remember being told about the results of the process and they told me that they were certain I had autism spectrum disorder. It didn't exactly take me by surprise, but it was quite a strange time for me because there were worries, like me thinking people would treat me differently, and that I'd get bullied for it. But I also was quite relieved that I now knew, because it meant people could also

understand me better and I could understand myself at long last. When I got diagnosed it was like a weight off my shoulders. It gave me a reason why I felt and behaved the way I did. I could really know who I was at last. Getting diagnosed stopped me hating myself because I understood myself better and didn't have that constant question in my mind asking why I was like this.

Autism affects people in different ways. Does it help you understand your own – and other autistic people's – behaviour?

Now that I have that label it actually helps me with finding solutions to my problems. I can spot and connect well with people with ADHD and autism – it's like a special gang that I wasn't a part of before.

What would you want other parents to know if they are concerned about their child and wondering if they should take them to a doctor?

I would 100 per cent go for it, it will always be better in the long run to know who you are. If I didn't have my diagnosis I wouldn't be where I am now. It's always the better option to look into it as much as you can at a young age.

GRAMMAR, PUNCTUATION & SPELLING ▶

1. Same spelling, different sound

Objective
To understand the different sounds that the letter-string 'ough' can spell.

What you need
Copies of *Can You See Me?*, dictionaries, photocopiable page 22 'Same spelling, different sound'.

What to do

- Together, read the paragraph in Chapter 2 beginning 'Outside the bedroom window'. Draw children's attention to the words 'enough' and 'through' and ask: *What do you notice about these words?* (They have the same 'ough' spelling.) Then compare how they sound (the 'ough' letter string is pronounced 'uff' in 'enough' and 'oo' in 'through').

- Explain that 'ough' is one of the trickiest spellings in English – it can be used to spell a number of different sounds. Ask: *Can you think of any words with the spelling 'ough'?*

- Write 'bought' on the board and ask the children to read it in their heads first. Then, ask them to read it aloud. Then repeat with all the words from the photocopiable sheet. Each time, ask: *What sound does the 'ough' make?* Say the sounds separately and then again with the whole word.

- Provide pairs with photocopiable page 22 'Same spelling, different sound'. Encourage them to pronounce the words to each other before deciding which group they belong in.

- After exploring these words, ask children to help you to create groups of 'ough' word cards to be displayed on your working wall.

Differentiation
Support: Provide an example from each group on the board for children to match the sounds.

Extension: Challenge children to use as many of these words they can in the same sentence.

2. Spelling tricky words

Objective
To learn to spell tricky words from the Years 5 and 6 spelling word list.

What you need
Mini whiteboards, sticky notes, felt-tipped pens.

What to do

- Call out the following words: 'embarrass', 'desperate', 'excellent'. Ask the children to repeat the words back to you. Ask: *How many syllables does each word have?* Ask children to say each word in different ways – a whisper, a roar, a funny voice.

- Ask children to write each word on a mini whiteboard. Ask children to show you their whiteboards at the same time so that you can quickly assess their ability.

- Display the correct spellings for each word and let children check and edit.

- Do the same with these three words: 'communicate', 'aggressive', 'curiosity'.

- Allow time for children to practise writing each word using the correct spelling – they could use sticky notes, felt-tipped pens or use chalk pens on black card.

- Ask for the meaning of each word. Encourage volunteers to use each word correctly in a sentence and relate the word to Tally's story. For example, 'Tally is desperate to fit in and be "normal"'. Again, focus on one word at a time. (Examples: 'Nell worries that Tally will embarrass her at school', 'Tally finds it difficult to communicate her feelings', 'Rupert the dog is thought to be aggressive', 'Tally has a curiosity about her friends and how they behave'.)

Differentiation
Extension: Ask children to play around with prefixes and suffixes for the focus words.

3. Powerful verbs

Objective
To discuss and explore the meaning of words in context.

What you need
Copies of *Can You See Me?*, dictionaries, photocopiable page 23 'Powerful verbs'.

What to do

- Re-read the beginning of Chapter 12 together (to 'to claim Layla for herself'), summarise events and discuss how Tally is feeling.

- Hand out photocopiable page 23 'Powerful verbs'. Tell children that you will read the extract and, as you read, you want them to spot verbs used. Ask them to highlight the verbs they have found ('walk', 'peels', 'follows', 'hear', 'talking', 'floats', 'grits', 'tries', 'focus', 'taped', 'stop', 'flooding').

- Discuss the verbs children have found and correct any inaccuracies.

- Ask pairs to discuss together which three verbs that they feel are particularly effective, before completing the first column of the table. They then work together, using a dictionary, to find definitions for column 2.

- Explain that you are now going to consider the author's use of these particular verbs. Use the word 'peels' as an example. Ask children who have written about the word 'peels' to share their definition. Ask: *When are we more likely to hear this word?* (peeling fruit or vegetables) *How do we imagine Tally moving away from the lockers? Why is she moving in this way?* (Tally has tried to blend in by pressing her back to the lockers, she is slowly pulling away from the lockers like she is being peeled.) *Is it a good verb to use at this point in the story?* Discuss children's ideas and then model completing the final part of the table.

Differentiation
Support: Before beginning, ensure that most verbs from the extract are listed in simpler dictionaries. If not, provide definitions for children to match.

Extension: Ask children to write a different version of the paragraph, swapping the verbs for new ones. Explore the change in meaning.

4. Direct speech and reporting clauses

Objective
To integrate dialogue to convey character and advance the action.

What you need
Copies of *Can You See Me?*; create large speech bubbles with examples of speech from Chapter 12; make labels displaying the reporting clauses from the text.

What to do

- Share the speech bubbles and read them together. Ask: *Who says this in the story? What part of the story is it from? How are characters saying these words? How are they feeling?*

- Display the reporting clauses and insert them between the speech. Ask: *What effect does this have?*

- Read aloud the full extract from Chapter 12 (the scene in the changing rooms when a girl's leg touches Tally's arm).

- As a shared write, write this speech as it would appear in the story. Model correct punctuation of inverted commas and commas to separate the reporting clauses.

- Then, together, re-read Chapter 16 to 'the first time all day', where Tally remembers the sleepover. Focus on the last four paragraphs and point out that there is no direct speech but we can guess some words that were said and other words are reported. For example, look at 'whispered it', 'said it a bit louder', 'it came out a bit like a shout' and ask: *What do you think Tally said?* ('I want to go home.') Look at the second paragraph and agree what Layla said ('Please stay, Tally! The sleepover will be ruined if you're not here with us.')

- Ask children to write the dialogue for these paragraphs, using the correct punctuation. Then share children's work together, focusing on the punctuation.

Differentiation
Support: Provide dialogue for children to punctuate.

Extension: Children create their own dialogue for another event, using the correct punctuation.

5. Formal or informal?

Objective
To understand appropriate vocabulary to use for both formal and informal speech and writing.

What you need
Copies of *Can You See Me?*; photocopiable page 24 'Formal or informal?'

What to do

- Revisit the family trip to the restaurant in Chapter 19. Focus on the waiter's speech from 'May I politely suggest' to 'this kind of commotion'. Ask: *Is this formal or informal language?* Agree together the formal features (use of 'May I', 'politely suggest', 'better suited'; longer words such as 'establishment', 'clientele', 'commotion').

- Then read 'Things that help when I'm stuck' near the end of Chapter 19. Ask: *Is this formal or informal language?* (informal). Find the informal features (contractions and language: 'It's a bit like', 'squish', 'cos', 'when I do this stuff, 'OK', 'It's like I'm').

- Discuss together when formal and informal language are used (formal language: in writing, with people we don't know well, serious situations; informal language: diary, speaking with friends and family). Explain that some words can be used in both formal and informal situations, but it's important to know which words are definitely not suitable for specific situations.

- Provide pairs with photocopiable page 24 'Formal or informal?' Once they have completed the table, encourage them to discuss the situations listed and explain their reasoning by giving examples.

- As a class, ask children to share their thoughts about the words and situations and ensure that they are using the words 'formal' and 'informal' when providing reasons behind their thinking.

Differentiation
Support: Children work with fewer words.

Extension: Ask: *What are your thoughts about the word 'gross'? Is it formal or informal?* Investigate use of the word 'gross'. Ask: *What does it mean? Has it always meant this? What are its origins?*

6. Words in context

Objective
To identify how language, structure and presentation contribute to meaning.

What you need
Copies of *Can You See Me?*

Cross-curricular links
Science, relationships education

What to do

- Look together at Tally's diary entry and 'autism facts' from Chapter 3. Point out the words 'petrified' and 'trait' and explain them using everyday language. Ask: *Does the 'autism facts' section feel different to Tally's other diary entry? Explain why.* (technical medical language, explanations) Notice the subheading 'Demand avoidance' and how Tally explains its full name, 'Pathological Demand Avoidance', and what it means for her. Point out her descriptions of the physical effects of her autism. ('My heart starts racing', 'a ball of anxiety and fear knotted inside')

- Ask pairs to skim the book and note down other technical terms that Tally includes and explains. (For example, 'sensory', 'stimming', 'neurotypical', 'masking' – see the end sections of Chapters 1, 3, 5, 9, 16, 25.) Together, explore how these are scientific terms used to describe aspects of autism.

- Ask: *What scientific terms do you know?* (If necessary, provide subject areas to help prompt ideas, such as space, biology, computing, chemistry and so on.) Ask: *Where do you usually hear them?* (non-fiction books, textbooks, news articles, classroom) *Do you expect to find scientific/technical terms in a story?* Discuss any other stories the class or individual children have read that also contain technical or scientific terms.

- Ask: *What do you feel after reading these 'autism facts' passages?* Explore children's responses. Ask: *Do you understand Tally better? Are the authors right to include these details about autism? Do they improve the story?* Discuss opinions.

Differentiation
Support: Provide children with the relevant extracts.

Extension: Ask children to research further words linked to autism.

Same spelling, different sound

- Cut out the word cards and arrange them in groups according to their sound.

1. How many sounds have you found?

2. Which words were a challenge? Why?

3. Choose one word from each group and find it in a dictionary. Record the words and their definitions in your book.

4. Choose three words that you don't use very often. Write each one in a sentence, in your book.

bought	tough	enough
though	cough	thought
ought	thorough	plough
borough	nought	rough
although	bough	dough
brought	through	fought

Powerful verbs

- Read the extract from Chapter 12:

> The girls walk past and Tally peels herself away from the lockers and follows them. She can't hear what they're talking about, but the sound of Layla's laughter floats back down the corridor. Tally grits her teeth and tries to focus on the posters that are taped to the walls, but she can't stop the thoughts from flooding into her head.

- Choose three verbs from the extract and complete the table below.

Verb	Definition	Effect on the reader

Formal or informal?

- Tick to show whether the words are formal (F) or informal (I).

	F	I
trashed		
hey		
agreement		
favourite		
shouty		
OK		
pongs		
unpredictable		
glance		
nope		

	F	I
freakiness		
losers		
excellent		
disbelief		
weirdo		
gonna		
embarrass		
awful		
good		
stuff		

- Look at each situation below. Which words would be acceptable to use in each situation? Which would not be suitable to use? Explain why.
  - When talking to a doctor
  - At a party with your friends
  - In a whole-school assembly
  - In the park with your family
  - During a job interview
  - When making a complaint to the council

PLOT, CHARACTER & SETTING ▶

1. The Perpetual Problem of Tally

Objectives
To consider and evaluate different viewpoints; to infer characters' feelings.

What you need
Copies of *Can You See Me?*

What to do
- Read Chapter 2 to the children. Ask: *What is the chapter mainly about? What information do we find out about Tally? How is she feeling at this moment in the story?*

- Arrange children into groups. Tell them that you will re-read three of the most significant incidents from the chapter. Read from 'Tally's arms stay resolutely folded…' to '"They're stuck."' and 'She sniffs and lifts up her hands…' to '"I told you."' and '"I'm sorry for being such a problem…"' to 'disturbs the peace.' Ask children to make notes about Tally's actions and speech: *What does she do? What does she say, and how does she say it? What does this tell the reader about her feelings?*

- Ask children to share the information they have gathered with their group.

- Have a whole-class discussion. Ask: *Did people in your group have similar ideas? Did anyone write something that you hadn't considered? What did you find interesting? What do we know about Tally from these events?*

- Ask children to continue to work in groups but split into pairs. They are to combine their notes to write a short diary entry for this part of the story, as Tally.

Differentiation
Support: Share sentence starters and phrases that children can include, such as 'Today I had to…', 'Mum said…', 'It felt very…'.

Extension: Ask children to write a diary for Tally's first day at Kingswood.

2. Character perspectives

Objective
To explore the characters in the story and draw inferences from the text.

What you need
Copies of *Can You See Me?*, photocopiable page 29 'Character perspectives'.

What to do
- Tell children that they are going to gain a deeper understanding of Tally's family.

- Re-read Chapter 9 (from, '"I saw an ambulance outside earlier," says Nell…' to 'Mum stands up and walks across to the sink.'). The events are described from Tally's point of view. Explain that you are going to use Tally's descriptions as clues to get a full picture of how her autism affects her family and friends.

- Organise children into groups and hand out copies of the book and photocopiable page 29. Allocate each group a different family member and ask the children to find information about their family member in this part of the book. This includes speech, actions and Tally's descriptions of facial expressions, and so on.

- Ask children to write all the evidence they find about their character into the first two columns, copying relevant words and phrases.

- The children should then decide how the characters are feeling at this point in the story and add it to the final column.

- Bring the class back together and share their findings on each character.

Differentiation
Extension: Children use their evidence to write a short diary extract from the point of view of that character.

3. High School

Objectives
To participate in discussions about books; to draw inferences.

What you need
Copies of *Can You See Me?*

What to do

- Remind the children of events in Chapters 18 and 19 (Tally tells Mr King about Luke and the assessment paper; Tally and her family go out for a disastrous birthday meal).

- Re-read Chapter 20, from 'The bell is ringing…' to 'Layla groans'. Model reading with fluency and expression. Ask children to continue to the end of the chapter reading aloud in pairs, and practising correct fluency, expression and accuracy.

- Then focus on the final part of the chapter. Ask: *How does it make you feel?* (uncomfortable)

- List the characters involved in this part of the story (Tally, Luke, Layla, Lucy, Ayesha, Jasmine, Ameet). Ask: *When the group first 'meet up' by the door, how do Tally's friends treat her? Why? How does Luke treat Tally? What does he call her?* Focus on the part from 'Tally frowns. "But I didn't do anything to Luke…"' to '"…so stop trying to make excuses for her, Layla."' Unpick all the details surrounding Luke's actions and speech – such as 'explodes Luke', 'face going red', '"ratted on me"'. Ask children to use these clues to describe exactly how Luke is feeling at this moment in time. Record all children's ideas on the board.

- Then focus on Tally ('frowns', '"It wasn't *me*"', 'shakes her head') and ask children to record Tally's feelings at this precise moment.

- Ask children to choose either Luke or Tally and write a message to a friend about these events.

Differentiation
Support: Give children a list of the 'evidence' from the story to use in their messages.

Extension: Ask children to write a set of messages between Tally and Luke – each trying to explain their side of the story.

4. The importance of animals

Objective
To consider Tally's actions, thoughts and feelings.

What you need
Photocopiable page 30 'The importance of animals'; different coloured highlighters.

What to do

- Organise children into pairs and hand out photocopiable page 30 'The importance of animals'.

- Read through each extract on the sheet and explain that the children are going to think about the actions, thoughts and feelings in each one.

- Ask pairs to highlight actions, thoughts and feelings in three different colours – they can make a key for these on the sheet.

- They should consider the information they've highlighted in each extract. Ask: *How does Tally treat these creatures? What are the feelings involved? What does that tell the reader about her?* Ask children to record their ideas in the spaces next to each extract on the sheet.

- Ask children to answer these comprehension questions to enable them to gain a deeper understanding:
  - *Why is Tally's voice quiet when she is speaking near the worm?*
  - *Why is she worried about the worm?*
  - *What does: 'Her eyes prickle…' mean? What is happening at this point in the story?*
  - *Why is Tally feeling this way?*
  - *What does Tally mean when she tells Rupert to start 'following the rules'?*
  - *What are Tally's feelings about the muzzle?*

- Ask children to consider all the evidence. Ask: *Why does Tally feel such a close connection to Rupert?* (She sees herself in him.) *Why is she kind to the worm? How does Tally feel about all animals?* Encourage children to consider why animals are so important to Tally.

Differentiation
Support: Ask children to answer only the first three questions.

5. Exploring settings

Objective

To make comparisons within and across books.

What you need

Sets of cards with phrases linked to settings: the only rule is gravity; possibilities are endless; fresh, new; she is a warrior; it's my place; she is weightless and free; smells mouldy and wet; too bright, too noisy, too dirty; hidden in the darkness; the shadows wrap themselves around her like a mask; nobody can see her; I'm not scared; grey and gloomy and huge; it smells wrong; beeping noises, which make Tally's pulse speed up; cold, sharp smell.

What to do

- Tell children that they are going to think about settings. Tally is very sensitive to her surroundings and the setting often has a substantial impact on her wellbeing.

- Together, list all the settings in the story. Ask: *How does Tally feel in each of these settings? Can you provide evidence to support your ideas?*

- Focus on the changing room and the hospital. Read the relevant parts of the story to the class (Chapters 12 and 28). Then focus on the shed (Chapter 1) and the dark street (when Tally is hunting for Rupert) in Chapter 27.

- Hand out copies of the cards and ask groups to organise them according to 'positives' and 'negatives'. Ask: *Which setting is this? What feelings are involved in this part of the story? Is it a positive or negative experience for Tally? How do you know?* Ask: *Which environments make Tally feel scared and uncomfortable? Which make her feel at peace?*

- Ask children to design a special room for Tally – a place that will help Tally feel at peace. They should label their design and explain the reasons behind their choices.

Differentiation

Support: Encourage children to consider what makes them feel happy and relaxed.

Extension: Ask children to include extracts from the story when explaining their choices for their design.

6. A calm place

Objective

To explore figurative language; to prepare poems to read aloud.

What you need

Copies of *Can You See Me?*, a copy of William Wordsworth's 'I wandered lonely as a cloud', Extract 1.

What to do

- Read 'I wandered lonely as a cloud' to the class. Explain any tricky words using everyday language. Discuss how the poet says the thought of the daffodils by the lake helps him to feel better (fills his 'heart with pleasure').

- Ask: *Do you have your own special place where you go to think or to feel calm and quiet?* Ask pairs to discuss and reflect on their own experiences.

- Share Extract 1 with children. Ask them to underline any information regarding Tally's view about the sky. Ask: *What are Tally's thoughts and feelings about the sky?* (Happy there are no rules, endless possibilities, a hint of something new/ fresh, Tally can be anyone, it is her special place, she can't think anywhere else, she feels weightless and free...)

- Then look together at other descriptions of the sky in the story (such as in Chapters 16 and 29).

- Explain that imagery is used to describe Tally's feeling of connection to the sky and how important it is to her. This can be called 'kinaesthetic imagery': language linked to physical action or natural functions to do with the body, such as heartbeat or a pulse. Encourage the children to find examples of this. (Tally can breathe properly; the sky feels like it is pushing down on her like a heavy blanket.)

- Share images of the sky. Ask children to use imagery to describe the sky as healing and peaceful. Note their ideas.

- Ask pairs to use the class notes to write and read aloud a short poem about the sky.

Differentiation

Support: Provide interesting adjectives and verbs.

Extension: Ask groups to practise and read aloud the Wordsworth poem.

7. Sights, sounds and smells

Objective
To explore the use of the 'rule of three' to describe characters and settings.

What you need
Copies of *Can You See Me?*, photocopiable page 31 'Sights, sounds and smells'.

What to do

- Ask if children have heard of the 'rule of three'. Explain it is a list of three words – often powerful adjectives and verbs – that writers often use to describe setting and characters.

- Hand out individual copies of photocopiable page 31 'Sights, sounds and smells'.

- Organise children into groups and explain that they are to read through the examples of the 'rules of three' used within the story. Can they decide which part of the story they are from? Designate a 'scribe' for each group and ask each group to appoint a 'speaker' who will report the group's ideas to the class.

- After 10–15 minutes, ask each speaker to share their groups' ideas and discuss. (You can confirm: A – Chapter 12, B – Chapter 17, C – Chapter 6, D – Chapter 12, E – Chapter 5, F – Chapter 29.)

- Ask the children to choose one set of words and consider the surrounding events in the story. Encourage them to discuss how the 'rule of three' description adds to the overall effect. Explain D as an example: *By describing the Maths classroom as 'hot and stuffy and stale', the writer is showing how trapped Tally feels. She stares out of the window at the sky, desperately wanting to feel '...the wind on her face'. As we know, the sky has healing properties to Tally.* Give children time to share their ideas.

- Bring the class back together and share their responses.

Differentiation
Extension: Ask children to choose a new set of three words and use them in a short piece of writing based on the story.

8. Nell

Objective
To ask questions to improve understanding.

What you need
Copies of *Can You See Me?*; create a 'role-on-the-wall' large blank outline of a person; large sticky notes – two sets, each a different colour; blank, A4-size speech bubbles.

What to do

- Display the 'role-on-the-wall' – explain this is Nell.

- With a partner, ask children to talk about Nell. Display questions to focus their discussion: *What do you think about Nell? What did you think about her at the beginning of the story and at the end of the story? Were there times when her actions annoyed you? Think of an event in the story when you agreed with Nell, and a time when you disagreed.* Children record their ideas on one colour of sticky note.

- Ask children to choose three or four of their most interesting ideas and stick them on the outside of the role-on-the-wall. Share some ideas with the class.

- Ask children to consider Nell's thoughts and feelings throughout the story. Ask: *How does Nell feel about the fair? How does Nell feel about Rupert? Can you think of times when she is kind to Tally? What about times when she isn't nice to Tally?* Children record their ideas on the second set of sticky notes.

- Share all ideas and encourage children to explain their answers using evidence from the text, even if they are not directly quoting the evidence. Ask volunteers to stick these sticky notes on the inside of the role-on-the-wall.

- Ask children to consider everything they have discussed. Then ask children to write questions for Nell on the blank speech bubbles. Share their questions and explain that we will consider the answers in a future activity (Talk about it, activity 2).

Differentiation
Support: Focus on just one event from the story that features Nell.

Extension: Ask children to begin to consider possible answers to the class's questions.

Character perspectives

• Use the table below to record evidence to show how your character is feeling.

Character:		
Thoughts	**Actions**	**How they feel**

The importance of animals

- Highlight Tally's actions, thoughts and feelings. Think about what this information tells you and write notes next to each one.

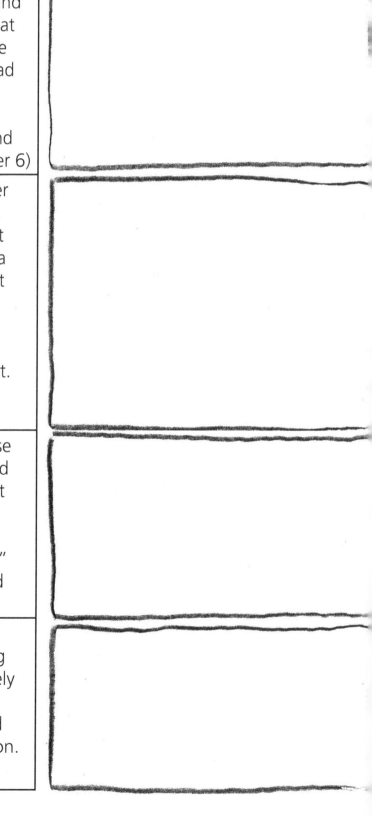

"It isn't gross. It's a living thing." Tally's voice is quiet as she crouches down and stares at the worm. It's the biggest that she's ever seen and it's lying right here on the path, where anyone could tread on it.
"You need to move, worm."
…she picks up the worm as gently and delicately as she possibly can. (Chapter 6)

Her eyes prickle and she scrunches her eyes up hard because tigers don't cry, not even when they're thinking about how terrible it is that Rupert has lost a leg and they can't bear to think about how sad he must feel about it.
"They don't get it," she says softly. "They all think you're angry and dangerous. But I know that you're not. You're just scared, aren't you, boy?" (Chapter 13)

"…you've got to work harder, because we're running out of time… Mum and Dad have had enough. Mum says that you've got to go, and then who will I have to talk to, hey? Stop being so selfish and start following the rules…" Rupert thumps his tail on the tiles and Tally laughs. (Chapter 22)

He's still wearing the muzzle – Mum insists that he has to keep it on during the day, which Tally thinks is completely cruel, even though Mum keeps trying to tell her that it doesn't hurt him and that he can still eat and drink with it on. (Chapter 20)

Sights, sounds and smells

- Which parts of the story are these words from?

A. Chapter_____

| mouldy | wet | sweet |

B. Chapter _____

| fizzing | churning | roaring |

C. Chapter _____

| mysterious | hot | dangerous |

D. Chapter _____

| hot | stuffy | stale |

E. Chapter _____

| pushing | barging | bickering |

F. Chapter _____

| maskless | autistic | proud |

- Choose one set of words. What effect does it have on the story?

_____

_____

_____

_____

_____

_____

_____

TALK ABOUT IT ▶

1. Freeze the moment

Objective
To participate in role play and improvisations.
What you need
Copies of *Can You See Me?*

What to do

- Explain that children will explore key moments in the story, thinking about different characters and how they react. Write these scenes on the board:

  - The makeover (Chapter 15): Tally, Ayesha, Layla, Lucy (make up two more friends – such as Jasmine and Aleksandra).

  - The restaurant (Chapter 19): Tally, Nell, Mum, Dad, people in restaurant.

  - The tiger mask in the drama studio (Chapter 23): Tally, Luke, Lucy, Layla, Ayesha, Aleksandra.

- For each scene, read the relevant part of the chapter. Before you begin reading, divide the class into groups of six and allocate each child a character. As you read, children must listen carefully and think about their characters' actions and feelings at that specific moment. If possible, also read Tally's diary extract linked to the scene. (Such as 'I keep trying to forget about it, but then I have a flashback of everyone crowding round me…'.)

- Each group will then create a 'freeze' of the scene.

- Give time for children to create their scenes. When they are ready, count down '3…2…1' and children must freeze. Choose different characters to focus on and tell children that when you tap them on the shoulder, they have to voice their character's thoughts at that moment in time.

- Afterwards, discuss their experiences. Ask: *How does it feel to put yourself in the 'shoes' of a character from the story?*

Differentiation
Extension: Ask children to reflect on their own experiences when discussing character thoughts and feelings.

2. Nell and Tally

Objective
To participate in role play and improvisations.
What you need
Copies *of Can You See Me?*, 'role-on-the-wall' from Plot, character & setting activity 8, photocopiable page 35 'Nell and Tally'.

What to do

- Review children's ideas from the role-on-the-wall activity from Plot, character & setting activity 8. Ensure they have a good understanding of the work produced during this activity. Tell children that they will further explore the character of Nell and her relationship with Tally.

- Organise children into pairs. One should play the part of Nell and the other an interviewer. The interviewer will ask 'Nell' the questions from the speech bubbles.

- Walk around the class and encourage pairs who are working particularly effectively to share their interview with the class.

- Ask children to consider events in Chapter 27, when Tally insists on looking for Rupert. Read up to 'And then she steps out into the night'.

- Ask pairs to act out the part of the story where Tally insists that she must find Rupert and Nell insists that they follow the rules. Allow time for discussion and practice. Again, watch the children as they rehearse and pick effective improvisations for a class performance.

- Ask children to complete photocopiable page 35 'Nell and Tally'. They can use the beginning of the sheet to record particularly effective extracts from their improvisations.

- Review children's findings and add new information to the role-on-the-wall.

Differentiation
Extension: Ask children, *How do you know?* to encourage the use of evidence to support their ideas and opinions.

3. Quote this

Objective
To discuss quotes from the story.

What you need
Photocopiable page 36 'Quote this'.

What to do

- Organise children into groups and explain that you will be exploring some quotes from the story. The quotes will be from a combination of the story itself, Tally's diary entries and Tally's information about autism.

- First, read each quote from photocopiable page 36 'Quote this'. Ask children to consider: *What part of the story is this from? What is happening at this moment in time? Who is involved?*

- Provide each group with the photocopiable sheet. Ask them to cut out each quote and discuss it. Display the following questions on the board to help their discussions: *What are your views about this quote? Why? How does it make you feel? Why? What part of the story is it from? Can you remember? Talk about the language used – any powerful adjectives or verbs? Does this quote remind you of anything in your experience? (something in your life? something from a book or a TV programme?)*

- Circle round the groups during the discussions, noting particularly interesting comments that you would like to use when reviewing the learning. Ask children involved if they are happy to contribute to a whole-class discussion.

- Ask groups to order the quotes from the most to the least effective – what are the reasons behind their choices?

- Review thoughts and opinions about each quote as a whole class. Use the volunteers spotted earlier. Refer to language used, talk about how powerful these quotes are and how our own experiences add to our understanding of texts read.

Differentiation
Support: Provide fewer, simpler quotes from the sheet and discuss their contexts.

4. Is Luke a bully?

Objective
To articulate and justify answers, arguments and opinions.

What you need
Copies of *Can You See Me?*

Cross-curricular link
PSHE

What to do

- Explain that you are going to think about Luke. Read extracts from the story where Luke is being unkind to Tally (Chapters 12, 14, 17, 18, 20). Ask children to make notes while you read, considering Luke's actions, thoughts and possible feelings.

- Ask children to share their notes with a partner and then discuss as a class.

- Tell children that they are going to further discuss Luke's behaviour and possible motivations, exploring why he might act the way he does. Split the class into two groups: one group will focus on Luke as a bully; the other group will focus on Luke as a person who is misunderstood.

- Display questions on the board for all to discuss, thinking about their group's viewpoint: *How does Luke feel about Tally? How does Tally feel about Luke? How does he make other children feel? Does Luke have any 'real' friends? Is Luke a bully? Is he happy? Why did he steal the assessment paper form Mr King's desk? Why did he wear Tally's tiger mask?*

- After an allocated amount of time, ask volunteers to share the main points of their discussion. Record on the board under headings of 'Bully' and 'Misunderstood'. Ask children to consider the viewpoints of the 'opposite' group.

- Finally, ask children: *What advice would you give to Luke?* Discuss and share ideas.

Differentiation
Support: Provide sentence starters for the discussion such as 'I think Luke doesn't understand…', 'I think Luke has his own problems…'.

Extension: Encourage more confident learners to provide evidence to support their reasoning. Can they consider other parts of the story that you have not mentioned?

5. Finding out more

Objective
To ask relevant questions to develop understanding.

What you need
Copies of *Can You See Me?*, Photocopiable page 37 'Finding out more'.

What to do
- Organise children into pairs and tell them that you are going to consider what they have found out about Tally's autism. Work completed during this activity will prepare children for Activity 6.

- Provide pairs with photocopiable page 37 'Finding out more'. Ask: *What did you already know about autism before you read the book?* Ask the children to discuss and make notes on the sheet, before discussing as a class.

- Ask: *How does the story inform the reader about Tally's autism?* (Tally's diary entries and 'autism facts') *What can children remember about Tally's autism?* (It is important to differentiate – as Tally does in the story – and support the fact that no autistic people share exactly the same experiences. In her interview, see Extract 4, Libby Scott said she felt that she was in a 'special gang'. This is a good way to approach the subject.)

- Ask children to complete the second part of the photocopiable sheet in their pairs.

- Tell children that they will now ask questions to find out more. Model considering information that you know already, and then asking a question that would help you to find out more (For example, 'Tally says that when she has a 'meltdown', her mum can help to calm her down. What does her mum do to help her feel calm?')

- Give children time to consider and discuss their questions and write them on the sheet.

- Ask children to share their questions with the class.

Differentiation
Support: Children write and draw diagrams/pictures to share their information.

Extension: Ask children to research Libby Scott online and find out more about her experiences with autism.

6. Tally's autism

Objective
To participate in presentations.

What you need
Copies of *Can You See Me?*, Photocopiable page 37 'Finding out more' completed in activity 5, index cards.

What to do
- Ensure children are working in the same pairs as for the previous session and hand out their completed photocopiable sheets. Explain that children will be using their previous work to give a presentation.

- Ask children to read their notes and questions. Place each pair with another pair to create groups of four. Ask children to share all their information.

- The groups should attempt to answer their questions, even if their answers involve model verbs such as 'might' or 'could' as they can't be certain.

- Each group should prepare a presentation about Tally's autism and her experiences. Give time to decide what they will say and who will say it. They can use the index cards as a memory aid for when they give the presentation. Write the following on the board to help groups focus their work: *Tally writes about autism 'pros and cons' – could you organise your information like this? What 'special' words will you be using? Can you tell the class their meaning? Can you link in extracts from the story to help explain some of your information? Are there some questions that you haven't been able to answer? How might you find the answers?*

- Each group will perform their presentation to the class.

- Talk about all the presentations. Ask: *Did any group present information that you had forgotten about or present new information that has taught you something?*

Differentiation
Support: Provide information for children to arrange into a presentation.

Extension: Ask children to research their questions online.

Nell and Tally

- Record some of the speech from your improvisations in the boxes.

Tally	Nell

Which character did you play? _____

What new things did you discover about your character?

_____

_____

_____

_____

_____

- Ask a question that will take your understanding further.

_____

_____

 **Quote this**

"I think I might make my own normal now." (Chapter 29)

'Actually, the more I think about it, the more I reckon that a lot of the cons of autism are not really caused by autism but by how other people react to it. I really do.' (Chapter 9)

'…but what if there are other kids in year seven who are different too and nobody has ever told her?

What if she isn't the only one?' (Chapter 21)

"No wonder you like him [Rupert] so much – you're both broken." (Chapter 14)

'…she walks across the room and looks in the mirror, staring at the strong, powerful creature in front of her. At the brave, magnificent Tiger Girl who doesn't feel pain and doesn't get hurt and doesn't worry about what other people think of her.' (Chapter 13)

'"Can you see me?"

She used to ask this question all the time when she was younger. Every time she put on the mask. And she was never quite sure what she wanted the answer to be. Whether it was better to be hidden or to be seen. Whether it was better to be Tiger Girl or Tally.' (Chapter 13)

'The sky is grey and heavy, but somewhere up there, beyond the clouds, is a glorious ceiling of blue, stretching as far as the eye can see.' (Chapter 29)

Finding out more

• Work with a partner and write what you already know about autism.

_____

_____

_____

_____

_____

• Use your copy of *Can You See Me?* to find information about Tally's autism and write it below.

Pros	Cons

• Ask questions to find out more:

_____

_____

_____

_____

GET WRITING ▶

1. A letter of advice

> **Objective**
> To identify audience and purpose for writing.
>
> **What you need**
> Copies of *Can You See Me?*
>
> **Cross-curricular link**
> PSHE

What to do

- Together, re-read Chapter 13 from '"It's everything!" screams Tally. "And I am not *upset*! I am *hurt*…"' to the end of the chapter.

- Ask children what they think about Tally and Rupert both being behind a mask. Tally asks, 'Can you see me?' Ask children for their opinions on Tally's contemplation about whether it is better to be hidden or seen – 'Whether it was better to be Tiger Girl or Tally.'

- Explain that they are going to write a letter of advice for Tally at this point in the story, considering what they have learned about her autism and how it affects her relationships with her family and friends. Ask children to think about the ending of the story – can they use this to help Tally feel better? Ensure that children know the correct format to use when writing a letter (how to begin, how it should end, layout).

- Ask them to skim through the text to find Tally's diary entries and 'Pros and Cons' which may help. Suggest that, if they wish, they can use some of their own experiences to help Tally.

- End the lesson by sharing some of the children's letters and discussing interesting advice that children have given.

> **Differentiation**
> **Support:** Allow children to copy words and phrases from the book, and even provide some if necessary.
>
> **Extension:** Encourage children to write in their own words, even if they are using information from the story.

2. A conversation

> **Objective**
> To write narratives using character dialogue.
>
> **What you need**
> Copies of *Can You See Me?*

What to do

- Re-read Chapter 17 from 'The next day isn't' to 'Now do us all a favour and disappear'.

- Focus on the dialogue. Point out the reporting clauses to the children: 'The words die on her lips', 'gasps Lucy', 'staring at Layla', 'snaps Luke', 'mutters Layla'. Talk about how the reporting clauses bring extra information to the scene – the reader uses these to infer character thoughts and feelings.

- Ask groups to discuss the impact of these phrases, one at a time, and then feed back their ideas to the class. For example, Luke 'snaps' because he knows that they don't have much time left and he doesn't want to get caught.

- Remind children how to punctuate dialogue using inverted commas and commas to separate reporting clauses.

- Explain that they are going to imagine the conversation between the other characters after Tally 'turns and stumbles' out. Discuss together what they might say ('"Did Weirdo Adams see me take the paper?" says Luke'; '"Tally's OK, Luke. She won't tell," pleads Layla'). Ask children to write the dialogue and use reporting clauses to give more information about the characters' thoughts and feelings. The story is written in the present tense – children could choose to use the past tense if they find this easier.

> **Differentiation**
> **Support:** Provide phrases that children can use ('shouts Luke as he curls his fist', 'mutters Layla').
>
> **Extension:** Ask children to write in the present tense and to use a thesaurus to include more interesting vocabulary.

3. Tiger mask

Objective
To evaluate and edit by proposing changes to vocabulary.

What you need
Copies of *Can You See Me?*, Photocopiable page 41 'Tiger mask', thesauruses, a tiger mask (optional).

What to do
- If possible, display a tiger mask at the front of the classroom – or wear it as the children enter!
- Organise children into groups and explain that they will be focusing on the tiger mask in the story. Ask groups to share their ideas and memories of the mask with each other and then discuss as a whole class. Encourage them to remember how Tally feels when she's wearing the mask – and how other people respond to it (Nell, her friends, the waiter in the restaurant).
- Hand out photocopiable page 41 'Tiger mask'. Allow several minutes for children to record their initial ideas using the prompts on the sheet. Share some ideas.
- Explain that they are going to write a description of the mask. Ask pairs to discuss their notes together and encourage them to be creative in their descriptions, referring to the senses and using interesting adjectives ('fiery orange with jagged black slashes', 'safe darkness', 'smells of Tally's fruity hand cream'). Ask them to continue to plan on the sheet.
- Children then write their first draft.
- Ask pairs to read their drafts to each other and suggest alternative adjectives to improve their descriptions. Provide thesauruses for them to refer to.
- Spend time working with children on proofreading and editing their piece.

Differentiation
Support: Direct children to relevant passages from the story to help prompt ideas (Chapters 13, 19, 23, 28). Provide a list of adjectives children can choose from to describe the mask.

Extension: Encourage children to use the 'power of three' in their descriptions.

4. Animals are good for you!

Objective
To create a poster for a specific audience and purpose.

What you need
Photocopiable page 42 'Animals are good for you!'

What to do
- Ask: *How does Tally feel about animals in the story?* Remind children of Plot, character & setting activity 4 and their discussions about the importance of animals for Tally. Discuss how she makes huge efforts to save the worm and how important Rupert the dog is to her. Agree that animals have a positive effect on Tally.
- Arrange children into groups and hand out photocopiable page 42 'Animals are good for you!'. Read through the information given about Meadows Farm and Animal Sanctuary. Ask for children's opinions about the poster (it is not very interesting).
- Give children time to discuss the following and ask a scribe in each group to record their ideas: *What is wrong with this poster? Talk about the information and how it looks to the reader. How would you improve it? What information do you need to keep? Is there any information you could add? How would you make sure that the farm receives lots of visitors?*
- Discuss the purpose of the poster, the audience and the format.
- Ask pairs to highlight and annotate the poster to improve it. They may add pictures, captions, speech bubbles – whatever they think will improve the poster.
- Share all children's ideas.
- Ask children to create their own, improved poster in pairs.

Differentiation
Support: Place copies of 'successful' posters on desks for children to use as 'What a good one looks like' (the subject of the posters needn't be related).

Extension: Ask children to give a mini presentation about their edits of the original poster and the changes they made.

5. Writing creatively

> **Objective**
> To practise writing ideas down quickly, using vocabulary previously explored.
>
> **What you need**
> Photocopiable page 43 'Writing creatively'.

What to do

- Explain that the children will be having a go at 'free writing'. They will choose a selection of words from different categories and then write a paragraph or short piece using them. The piece should be related to *Can You See Me?* but can be about any event or character. It can be written in the first or third person.

- Hand out photocopiable page 43 'Writing creatively' and read through it with the children.

- Model choosing one word from each category and quickly writing ideas that come to mind. For example: 'Behind my **tiger mask** there is **silence**. I **sniff** the familiar **rubbery** smell and feel at ease. All is calm. I love my tiger mask. I got it when I was three years old. I remember putting it on at the **fairground**, staring at the **sky** and feeling calm'.

- Model making the occasional mistake and tell children that you will go back and edit later. Say that you have noticed that you used the word 'calm' twice. This is another thing for you to address later. Point out that your punctuation is mostly correct and encourage them to use punctuation to the best of their ability.

- Give children time to free write. Let them know that you will spend a different lesson proofreading and editing so you only advise they read through to help them check mood/tone/atmosphere of their piece.

- Finish the lesson by asking volunteers to read out their writing.

> **Differentiation**
> **Support:** Write words from the list in longer phrases or sentences to scaffold the writing and help give ideas.
>
> **Extension:** As children write, encourage interesting vocabulary choice. Share lists of words that they may like to use ('overwhelming', 'torment', 'judgement', 'joyous', 'heartsick').

6. Tally's diary

> **Objective**
> To write in the first person when writing a diary entry.
>
> **What you need**
> Copies of *Can You See Me?*

What to do

- Read several examples of Tally's diary entries to the class. Remind children that these were written by Libby Scott when she was 11 years old. They are based on her own diary entries and advice that she wrote for her parents. Ask children if they have read other books that are written as diaries. (For example, *The Diary of a Killer Cat* by Anne Fine, *Diary of a Wimpy Kid* by Jeff Kinney and *Dandelion Clocks* by Rebecca Westcott.)

- Point out the use of first-person pronouns ('I'/'we', 'me'/'us', 'my'/'mine', 'our'/'ours'). Explain that the use of first person is particularly effective as it allows the writer to share the main character's thoughts and feelings. It can make the reader feel like they know them. *Can You See Me?* is written using a combination of both first person and third person.

- Talk about tense. Share an extract from the main body of the story and one of the diary entries. Ask: *What tense have they been written in?* (present) Explain that the present tense adds an immediacy to the story – the reader feels like they are there with characters as events are unfolding. The diary entries give the reader an extra insight into Tally's character.

- Tell children to choose from one of these events in the story: the Sky Dancer ride at the fair (Chapter 7), the makeover from hell (Chapter 15), the restaurant (Chapter 19), looking for Rupert (Chapter 27). They then write a diary entry as Tally to describe the event from her point of view.

> **Differentiation**
> **Extension:** Ask children to bring in 'autism facts' at the end of their diary, as it is in the book, using what they have learned.

Tiger mask

- Look at the table below. Write words and phrases that you can use to describe the tiger mask.

Colours	Smell
Texture	**Shapes**

Any other ideas:

Animals are good for you!

- Read the poster below. What do you think about it? How could you make it better?

Come to our farm, it's really good.

Meadows Farm
We are also an animal sanctuary because we love animals.

You can feed the animals and spend time with them.
We have pigs, goats, cows, llamas, guinea pigs, hamsters,
ducks, geese, sheep, chickens, horses, donkeys, rabbits.

We have a gift shop and toilets and a play area for small
children, including small tractors to drive on.

We have a large play barn for older children with rope swings
and a zip wire.

Meadows Farm, Sunnyside Lane, Framington, FB6 9RH

In the nice countryside

You can get ice cream, gifts.

Have fun and learn.

Writing creatively

Choose one item from each list. Use them to create a short passage of writing related to *Can You See Me?*

Object	Sound
tiger mask	roaring
Sky Dancer	fizzing
ice cream	shouting
uniform	Taylor Swift's latest song
squishy	laughter
history test	whirring of a hand dryer
letter of apology	silence
Place	**Smell**
kitchen	sweet
shed roof	mouldy
drama studio	dirt
changing room	fresh
school corridor	smokiness
the pavement	musty
fairground	rubbery
Action	**Nature**
imagining	sky
flapping arms	storm
screaming with fright	stars
jiggling her feet	worm
shaking her head	rain
sniffing	clouds
whispering	garden
watching *Peppa Pig*	Rupert

ASSESSMENT ▶

1. Mrs Jarman

Objective
To listen and respond appropriately.

What you need
Copies of *Can You See Me?*

What to do

- Explain to the children that they will listen to a text and then demonstrate their understanding by completing an activity based on what they hear.

- Set the scene by asking children to describe Mrs Jarman and specific events that have occurred in the drama studio. Tell them that they will be looking at the first time the reader meets Mrs Jarman and exploring Tally's conflicting thoughts about her. Give children time to have an initial discussion about the character.

- Before reading, write on the board: *What does Mrs Jarman do? What does she say? What does Tally think about Mrs Jarman at first? How does Mrs Jarman confuse Tally? Why does Tally change her opinion of Mrs Jarman?*

- Read aloud Chapter 5, modelling fluency and expression. Allow time for a discussion of the questions in groups and encourage children to note ideas.

- Check the children's understanding of various words in context by asking them to think of synonyms for these words: 'spherical', 'ice-breaker', 'steely'.

- Ask the children to either write a detailed description of Mrs Jarman or list the events of the chapter in order with as much detail as possible.

- Assess the children's ability to listen, retrieve information and demonstrate their understanding of the character and the events surrounding her.

Differentiation
Support: Children draw a labelled picture of Mrs Jarman using simple evidence from the text.

Extension: Ask children to re-read other chapters where Mrs Jarman appears in order to extend their descriptions.

2. Rules for being normal

Objective
To discuss their understanding and explore the meaning of words in context.

What you need
Copies of *Can You See Me?*, photocopiable page 47 'Rules for being normal'.

What to do

- Read Chapter 22 together, up to '...that isn't a very nice place to be.' Model reading with fluency and expression and ask for volunteers to read aloud to demonstrate their abilities.

- Read the questions on photocopiable page 47 'Rules for being normal' together. Refer to question 1 and model highlighting key words in a retrieval question and then scanning to locate the correct information in the text.

- Remind children of how to check for meaning if they are unsure of a specific word (read in context) and explain that you want them to answer the questions in complete sentences.

- Model a second 'practise question' that requires inference: *Why does Tally feel that she would not be able to go into the canteen without Layla?* Model thinking about what we have learned about Tally so far and her relationship with Layla. Share thoughts on how Tally feels generally about high school. Then answer: 'Tally does not want to go into the canteen without Layla as it is a scary place to her. It will be noisy and filled with people. Layla is her best friend and understands Tally's autism. Tally feels safe when she is with Layla'.

- Give children time to answer the questions.

- Check the children's answers to assess their comprehension skills.

Differentiation
Support: Allow children to answer without using full sentences.

Extension: Challenge children to create their own questions about an event to take their understanding further.

3. Finding poems

Objective
To demonstrate understanding of how word choice can affect meaning and imagery.

What you need
Copies of *Can You See Me?*, copies of Extract 1, dark-coloured felt-tipped pens, examples of found poetry.

What to do

- Explain to children that they will be creating 'found poems' (poems that are created by finding words and phrases in a text). These are sometimes called 'blackout poems'.

- Hand out Extract 1 and read it together. Ask children about the part of the story it is from (the first chapter). Ask: *What is happening? What are the feelings involved? How did you feel as a reader when you first read this?*

- Ask them to re-read the extract, finding words and phrases that they believe are particularly powerful and circling them. The aim is for these words and phrases to reflect the thoughts/feelings/ideas/in this part of the story.

- Share examples of found poetry so the children get an idea of how creative they can be. Some poems can just involve blacking out all the words except the 'found' words and phrases. Children could also 'pull out' chosen words and phrases and re-write them as a poem, if they wish. Another choice is to circle the words with a shape like a cloud, a house or a mountain. The irrelevant words can be blacked out with a picture drawn over the top of them.

- Ask children to share their poetry and talk about the reasons behind their word choices.

- Assess children's choice of vocabulary and their understanding of the effect they have created.

Differentiation
Support: Children circle words within the text and black out the rest or create felt-tipped designs to hide them.

Extension: Children 'pull out' the words and re-arrange to create a particular effect or mood.

4. Understanding character

Objective
To consider viewpoints of different characters within a text.

What you need
Copies of *Can You See Me?*

What to do

- Organise children into groups and tell them that they will be writing in-role as one of the characters from the story.

- Ask children to discuss the different characters and pick one that they would like to be.

- Explain that a monologue is a long speech by one character that often includes them describing their thoughts and feelings. Tell children that they are going to write a monologue for their character at a chosen point in the story. Children then pick an event from the book where their character is important. They re-read this part of the story and take notes to inform their writing. Notes should be focused on feelings involved, actions, dialogue, description of facial expression and body language.

- Model how to begin a monologue, reminding children that the language they use can be informal. For example, Luke might say: 'I can't believe what that awful girl just said about my mum and dad. I mean, I know I said something a bit like that, but she shouldn't have said that. I can't believe it. She knows about my mum. I've even forgotten to be angry because I feel…well, I don't even know how I feel. I don't think I've ever felt like this before. I just stare at her. At her stupid face.'

- Give children time to play around with their monologues – they can choose the tense that they write in but are to write consistently in the first person.

- Assess children's understanding of character and their use of first person in writing.

Differentiation
Support: Children could be presented with character pictures and thought bubbles, or draw their own, to record their character's thoughts and feelings.

Extension: Challenge children to write as an adult character – for example, Mrs Jarman.

5. The hospital

Objectives
To listen and respond appropriately; to summarise the main ideas.

What you need
Copies of *Can You See Me?*

What to do

- Discuss events in Chapter 28, when the family visit Dad in hospital. Ask: *How does Tally feel in the hospital? Can you remember why?*

- Write these phrases on the board and discuss the mood they create at this point in the story: 'panting for breath', 'creepy maze', 'beeping noises', 'pulse speed up', 'terrifying', 'hectic', 'shallow breaths'.

- Agree that Tally is petrified of the hospital – link in what the children now know about Tally's autism.

- Tell children that you are going to read an extract from this chapter. As you read, you want them to consider what the main idea is. Read from 'Nell leads the way' to 'Her arms start to flap and she lets them.'

- Ask children to discuss their ideas for the main idea of the extract. It's important to consider how frightened Tally is and how, despite this, she decides to take off the mask and be herself.

- Ask children to write a paragraph in their own words to summarise the extract. Assess children's ability to retell important events in the story.

Differentiation

Support: Ask children to list key words to help remember the details as they listen. They can also use ideas presented by other children during the beginning of the lesson.

Extension: Encourage children to go a little deeper with their writing. Tell them that it is more of an analysis. Ask children to consider the importance of this extract to the whole story. Encourage them to make links between this event and Tally's use of the mask in previous chapters and also to consider her changing thoughts about her autism.

6. Developing settings

Objective
To describe settings, characters and atmosphere.

What you need
Photocopiable page 31 'Sights, sounds and smells', thesauruses.

What to do

- Organise children into groups. Refer to Plot, character & setting activity 7 and photocopiable page 31 'Sights, sounds and smells'. Remind children of the powerful descriptions within the story that are often written as a 'rule of three'.

- Together, write a list of settings from the story: the PE changing room, the drama studio, the shed roof, the corridors of the high school, Tally's bedroom, the hospital.

- Connect each 'rule of three' on the sheet to each setting (not all these settings will link to a set of words on the sheet). Jot notes on the board and ask children if they have any ideas for one of the settings that you can add.

- Allocate a setting per group and ask children to discuss words and phrases that would best represent their setting – they may also copy words from the book. Children need to consider how to create atmosphere and must refer to the senses.

- Share ideas and ask children to add to them using a thesaurus.

- Ask children to consider their words and phrases. Ask: *What words/phrases would work particularly well as a 'rule of three'?* Give time for children to independently play around with their word choices.

- Ask children to write a detailed description of their setting. Challenge them to bring in some of their 'rule of three' ideas to create a specific atmosphere.

Differentiation

Support: Provide children with a list of words and phrases. Ask them to consider which words are suitable and which are not suitable for their description. Assess their choices, which will reflect their understanding of the story.

Extension: Ensure children use a range of word and sentence types in their description.

Rules for being normal

- Read Chapter 22 and then answer these questions in your book.

1. How does Tally avoid splashing soup down her chin?

2. Why is Tally wearing her tiger mask?

3. Who does Tally visit when everyone has left the kitchen?

4. How does Tally feel about Rupert?

5. How does being with Rupert make Tally feel?

6. Why do Tally's parents want to send Rupert to a dog shelter?

7. What is rule number one?

8. '...pretend to be someone else. Someone who isn't different.' Why is it important for Tally to teach Rupert this rule?

9. What does Tally do when she is happy?

10. How does the writer describe the calm feeling that Tally feels when Rupert looks at her?

11. Why is it important for Rupert to be 'normal'?

12. Describe Tally's relationship with Rupert. Why does she like him so much?

13. As a reader, what do you think about this part of the story?

SCHOLASTIC

READ & RESPOND

Available in this series:

978-1407-15879-2

978-1407-14224-1

978-1407-16063-4

978-1407-16056-6

978-1407-14228-9

978-1407-16069-6

978-1407-16070-2

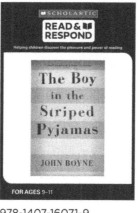

978-1407-16071-9

978-1407-14230-2

978-1407-16057-3

978-1407-16064-1

978-1407-14223-4

978-0702-30890-1

978-0702-30859-8

To find out more,
visit www.scholastic.co.uk/read-and-respond